Broad Sympathies in a Narrow World:

The Legacy of W. E. B. Du Bois

Broad Sympathies in a Narrow World:

The Legacy of W. E. B. Du Bois

Poems by
Sandra Stanton-Taiwo

BROADSIDE LOTUS PRESS
Detroit

First Edition
Printed in the United States of America

Cover Art by Christina Bennett

Front Cover Photo of W.E. B. Du Bois, c1919
by C.M. Battey, Library of Congress,
Washington, D.C.

Book Design and Layout by Leisia Duskin

NLM Award Series Editor
Gloria House

International Standard Book Number
9780-940713-26-052000

BROADSIDE LOTUS PRESS
Post Office Box 02011
Detroit, Michigan 48202
www.BroadsideLotusPress.org

This book is dedicated to my mother and father,
Elma Louise and James Ray Staton; my daughters,
Hannah-Isabella Oluseun Taiwo,
and Temitopeoluwa Louise Taiwo;
my mentor, Rose Marie Sherman,
and to all those poets who have inspired me,
including my friends
at the Furious Flower Poetry Center.

CONTENTS

DRAMA

FAMILY STUDIES

Like a broken bone inside a cast,
I crouch and wait.

Of the Passing

Unnatural,
when babies pitter patter
to paradise beyond parenting,
"so still he be
and he be there."

Nothing natural
when time escapes
"not dead, but escaped,"
before the sands fall
or eulogy calls
to report a past
that lasts.

"There be a there,"
naturally,
lest sanity
pitter patter to paradise
with thee.

Little Yolande's Blues

You hurt me as a child,
but I ain't a child no more.
You hurt me as a child,
but I ain't a child no more.
Now, this is my game,
and I'm the one keeping score.

Chiasmus

Daddy's daughter dotes
dubbing daughter two
daddy's name
reversed,
chiasmus
reparated,
reparented, after
wedding a daddy,
just like dear old dad.

You've seen how daughter
got turned around by dad.
Now see how dad
gets turned around
by daughter,
lifetime spent,
paying
for failing to be,
he nor thee,
left in a void,
like sacrificial maidens
cast
into angry volcanoes,
trapped
inside a cocoon
of a lava-less life,
failing to explode
to flight.

Cocoon

Inside this cocoon
I struggle to understand
the binding that limits my span.
Like a broken bone inside a cast,
I crouch and wait
to escape.

Feeling Nina Yolande I

Pregnancy hormones remained,
hovering
like smoke after a forest fire;
the ultra sound
found
a babyless pouch,
fluids flittered like ashes
over a furnace cooling down.

Decisively,
inevitably,
I return to emotional clearings,
tears searing sadness into closed casket funerals.
The fetus had fallen
like a single teardrop,
see through,
half fluid-filled bubble,
lima-like bean
floating
inside a stagnant bath,
eyes on each side,
of a child
never held in arms
but held,
like before the passing
of his first born,

a child not allowed
to grow full-sized,
but held,
under a smile,
for a while, until
projected memories fell
like tears, watering a fetus
uprooted to fragrance
that "there be a there."
"To a hope not hopeless but unhopeful."
"But the world shall end when I forget."
Here too,
the "little soul leapt
like a star that travels in the night."

Death proves universal
at any stage of living.

Feeling Nina Yolande II

Ain't I, too, a woman,
scorned,
doubly-conscious
of loving
and loathing
and sharing
in no man's land,
contempt and pity
on the same side of a coin
tossed away?

Ain't I, too, a woman,
"all life-long crying without avail?"
Scarred,
behind the veil,
a wedding veil,
trapped,
in loving
but loathed
when sharing,
one-sided,
in a house
alone
is not a home.

Nina Yolande's Lament
Haiku Series

Shirley's shadow blocked
the sunshine I should have sensed,
but I tasted first.

Our trees bore our fruit.
The children proved the best ones,
first one plucked away.

The second, like me,
failed to yield the juice you craved;
girl-children we stayed.

While, publicly, you
chastised time for limiting
gender blossomings,

privately, you stopped
gardens from overgrowing
in the home you watched

from afar, tended
by lectures spoken to all,
like fertilizer

killing bugs of hope,
expectations pulled like weeds,
before they all grow.

And I learned to know
single long stems stand alone,
away from gardens,

left to last so long,
till nourishment ceased to be,
and leaves fell like tears

dropping over years,
watching other planted buds
have their pollen sucked

and then plucked, like me
until the tree called Shirley
over-shadowed all.

'Bout Me

To Nina Yolande, the found,
and the younger Yolande, the lost

"You must not know 'bout me,"
Beyoncé bellows from the belly,
and every female's fellow
hears and fears.

She's Angela Davis
and insurrection
resurrecting a long-lost fervor
to fight.

She's right,
preaching to the masses
of broken-hearted misses
to stand up and see
the light.

Mama's been saying it for years:
there's more fish in that sea
of forgetfulness,
of sins begotten
and then forgotten,

for past cannot be lived again,
born again
in some reverse revival,
recycling hurts that knock
like an unworthy suitor

who courts
and then aborts
the girl who supports
the warts
of his deadly kiss.

Sleeping Beauty, Cinderella, and Snow White
were not right.
The prince will not come looking,
and if, by chance, he sees the girl,
he'll only see what she lets him see.

I am the one I want to see.
I find the princess in myself
and live.
I give myself the right
to fight.
I won't lie down
to wait for him
to come
to save the day.

By the time he values me,
I've left.

"You must not know 'bout me,"
'cause I know 'bout myself.

RELIGIOUS STUDIES

*...like Joshua, leading your people
to face giants....*

Home

Swing low,
sweet chariot.
Come and go,
Sweet Harriet,
into a new millennium.
Coming for to carry memory,
night riding
to the homes
of those who dream of divvying
human rights
in a new reality
against anti-Christian
hospitality.

Swing low,
sweet chariot.
Come to claim homestead,
forty acres squared,
in a land amnesiac.
"Those who cannot remember the past
are doomed
to repeat it."
But Du Bois stamped abolition
across the pages,
with codes like quilts to freedom.

Swing, swing, swing
low to cherish
a people labeled.
"How does it feel
to be a problem?"

Doubt

Doubt,
he learned from Crummell,
would feed on contempt,
like vultures
on bodies struggling to survive
the stench of decaying
surroundings;
feed like parasites
on race
to erase
one face of humanity.
Pity insanity,
and round off like double-dutch,
again and again,
hopping over hope.

Joshua

At twenty-five
you wielded pen
to send yourself out
like Joshua
to lead your people to face giants,
earning with Caleb-like camaraderie
the right to remain
in a land otherwise inhabited
by those who thought they stood too big
to confront the little man
with the big ego,
rejoicing,
as a strong man to run
the race.

Faith

Faith for you
framed a force
to be reckoned with,
a cause
that exposed
those
who chose
holier than thou status,
instructing others to be
less than or equal to
nothing
in a world spirit
that blew monopolies
like leaves in autumn storms,
clearing for inevitable change.
Faith for you
was the future you knew.

Revolution

His father had been a Haitian
or born there at least—
born
like a burden to be eased
like when he eased himself,
eased himself,
right out of Du Bois's life,
like a worm into a hole,
underground,
"not dead, but escaped,"
possibly for good reasons,
all unknown but,
nevertheless,
gone.

He is so like my ex,
Haitian
and paternal,
in a deadbeat kind of way,
when convenient, but
away,
even when around;
around
for the sex,
but not very committed
as I felt whenever I was with him,
committed,
institutionalized,
whenever I was with him;

with him, the one I knew,
knew in the biblical way,
intimately intimidated,
vexed by the ex
and the sex imposed
to produce
until reduced
into a hole.

I knew him
in the biblical way,
chastised for sins
omitted
and committed,
and he thought he knew me too,
nit-picking
till I, too, thought me crazy,
and I committed
to admit it.
He nit-picked my soul,
as if it had been a sweater filled with lint,
nit picking imperfections
of newfound usefulness,
of the naturally functional,
until substance dwindled,
too weak to escape.

He nit-picked
until I picked
a different sweater
with a different set of lint;

a different past soon passed,
a self-less soul,
an alter soul
alternately
altering me
into a self-made cocoon
when he was around
and into a man-made hole
when I was alone,
wondering what I left undone
this time
to collect all of that lint
again and again,
no matter what sweater I wore—
imperfections nit-picked
until my soul filled with holes,
traumatized
until the holes tore the whole
wholly apart,
apart from all I used to be,
apart from all I used to know,
isolated and alone,
sweater-less and exposed,
self-less,
until I took less,
"not dead, but escaped,"
no longer committed to the "committee
of that curious *tertium quid*
which we call public opinion."
I was better off
alone.

His father had been a Haitian,
apart but not a part,
born there but escaping here,
"not dead, but escaped"
when he rebelled,
and they rebelled,
and I rebelled,
to seize freedom by force,
as when the first black republic
rebelled,
like Desalines and L'Ouverture.

We took our sweaters back,
lint and all,
a past to call
and response,
to do with as we pleased,
to wear whenever we willed to wear.
We wore a willing war,

like Du Bois,
who waged a political war
and took his passport back,
never to come back
to this land
is my land,
this land is your land.

He left the land of history and
"lies agreed upon"
for a land where sweaters were made
to be worn
beautifully,
naturally,
unconditionally.

Du Bois,
who reversed his father's passage,
outliving his father
almost two to one,
survived.

HISTORY

Your drumbeat lives again.

Replaced

What would you say now,
Du Bois,
if you graced today,
when race
stands re/placed
by space, and
education is sold
to the highest tax-paying bidder;
where home ownership
deter/mines
educational fellowship,
shutting doors
to those who can't afford
space
in a race
replaced?

Black Man

Black man,
listen to the drums of your past,
beating out your name,
calling out your name.
You, black man,
from any of many a tribe
of Ghana or Mali or Songhai,
of people who valued the family—
nomadic, agricultural,
full of body, full of soul,
full of sense and spiritual.

First in much,
you
stood alone,
using iron when others used stone.
Full of dreams and visions, you,
from Vassa and Attucks and Banneker,
Wells Brown, Carver, and Dr. Drew,
Vesey and Turner and Walker's Appeal,
William Nell and William Sill,
fiery Du Bois and calm Booker T.,
militant Garnet and Marcus Garvey,
Johnson and Baldwin and Wright and Hughes,
writing the rights and lighting the fuse,
Adam, Colin, Mandela, McNair,
X, Malik, and all who would dare—
Benjamin Davis, Douglass, Hall,
Cuffee, Farmer, King, and all—
to name a few;

like you
black man,
who
graced the world with royalty,
crossed the world to slavery,
taught the world to be set free—
saw victory,
sees victory,
will see victory.

Drumbeat

To fiery Du Bois,
who,
in the midst of a war
against those who shot
when they didn't see the whites
of their I's,

wrote about the soul suppressed
in ways his eyes were trained to see,
to train those who were blinded by
a lie.

To you who died before the March,
and paced your own determined march
to the beat of a different drummer,
to fight a present
that confined your army
to a past.

To you,
who bound the past
and seized the future
with the drumbeat of your pen,

your drumbeat lives again.

Buffalo Soldier

For James Ray, Sr. (1939-2002)

You were my Buffalo soldier
from this other century, born
seventy-six years after the first ones
stopped the war-torn riding.

I smile when I think of you
and the memories you bequeathed.
Named for sacredness,
you fought in the one war
that actually supported you.
You marched behind buffers
and waxed the scuff off floors.

I remember how you showed me how
to make them go away.
You take them up the very same way
that you put them down, you'd say.
The rubber sole of the shoe that left its mark
can take it right back up again.
And then you showed me how,
and I watched the mark disappear
like lemonade on a hot summer day.

You stood firm in your convictions
and helped posterity
reach the dreams that you yourself had dreamed
or had never dreamed.

With your head held high,
you fought the fight worth fighting
and came back home with many bestowed honors
for being a strong black man,
who earned a living
by any means necessary.
You were much too proud
to sit and just do nothing.
Through snow you marched to get to work.
Your dreams were bigger than you,
for you knew
that after you were gone,
your work would still live on.
Your deeds would have been done,
but
the battles that you fought
and won
would someday make your future.

Determination was your gun,
persistence, your horse,
as you galloped
and protected
what was yours.

Spiral

In our spiral of history,
we swam through rivers of tears,
fighting emotional torrents
gushing against rocks of sanity,
that made no hiding place,

until arms and legs
ached and cramped,
and all we did
was fight,
hiding the pain
of birthing new life.

EDUCATION

You made a point to tell them they were good.

Contention

Contention
is what comes
on those little kitty feet,
purring just before you see
the claws,
and then moves in.

We live and learn through
Willie Lynch and
claw anyway,
labeled as a race
who are trained
to reflect color
rather than absorb valor.
If we must die,
let it not be
internally.

Culture

And the headline in the bad newspaper said
you people are in trouble
with the law
and with all those who support it
except you—
you
who planted seed,
for the crisis of the night.

You opened up the culture section
hidden in the middle,
where you formed a feature story,
like Adam out of mud,
breathing life into lifeless strokes,
molding clay into
Black folks
with soul
and you said,
"Out of the evil
came something
of good."

What's their worth?
You made a point to tell them
they were good,
cradling fruit multiplied,
and not aborted
by those who tried to headline
them as bad.

You fed the angry with your words,
writing refuges of sustenance
so they would not feed on bad
and then believe
that the wall paper of separation
stood high enough to hide the truth.

Natural

Part I: Summer
I, too, wore locks before,
and three years I had borne them
like a growing child,
like the ministry of Jesus, set aside
for sacrifice and
inevitable crucifixion.
And then I picked them out, the locks,
for people called me blasphemous
for not worshipping *Ras Tafari*,
for wearing locks
as a style,
for being too radical,
for seeming to smoke marijuana,
for seeming lesbian even; for,
though I loved myself some men,
I also had a past with men—
a past
like the woman at the well,

thirsty for water given
but not received,
stripped to crusty dryness,
parched,
with a past locked in place,
by other voices,
out of place,
condemning,
defining,
confining.

New growth is hindered
when dead strands twist like vines,
in unmonitored suffocation.
How can one kill the past
without cutting off the future?
The past can grasp,
like locks promising growth through painful pulling
of many strands into one,
like one who stands at the well,
who claims to be the one true vine
who turned the water into wine.
Grapes on vines mashed for wine?
Vines, like the past, exploit or support,
pending interpretation.

Part II: Fall
I, too, wore locks before,
and for months I did pick them out,
for a Haitian called them dirty,
a Haitian with a past of picking free.
Dirt is dirty, too, I said, but naturally
a must
for the growth of all that dares to live,
like slaves in ships,
uprooted and planted in some other land
suddenly
reach for liberty
out of the mud of
slavery;
like grandmothers locked in liberties
that were not their own,
who did not own their own bodies
or what their bodies did,
who owned not a thing
but the songs they sang.

Were they wearing locks as well?
And could the locks have set them free
from all the dirt of slavery?
The past has locks to be picked
away,
to be recalled
for a brighter day, after
inevitable crucifixion.

Memories lay
ready to be released,
with a savior
to be crucified
and then resurrected.
New growth sprouts entangled
with the unrelenting past,
not standing steadfast in liberty,
but bound
by a history of oppression
by men who think they own the world
because they plant their seed,
because they force their seed sometimes.
But sometimes is enough
to bow any woman down
into a fetal position,
afraid
to open up again,
afraid
to blossom for a bee
that stings.
Beginnings are hard to forget sometimes.

The past stands,
rooted in fragile memories;
but there comes a time to chop time down,
to uproot trees
that once provided shade in summer
but now must warm in winter.
The past transitions with death to life,
with the freedom seeds of memory.

Part III: Winter
I, too, wore locks before.
Then for seven years I went without,
without simplicity,
struggle without progress—

life, liberty, finances—
sweating under hairdryers,
paying for traumatic choices
not my own.
But I grew weary
for a past forgotten, and
after seven years,
returned to locks
for almost a decade,
until gray set in and the past grew heavy
once again.
And so again
I picked again.
For ten long months, I picked again,
like a prisoner behind bars
subdued by one strong lock to be picked.

I missed the feel of single hairs, free to shed
or stay,
free to twist and fight among themselves
like so many crabs in a bucket,
pulling one another down.
When I did not own my hair,
my mother straightened it,
just to have it go right back
like a rebellious child.
"Don't make me come in there," she'd say,
clutching her smoking comb
against the nape of my neck
like a handful of switches from the nearest tree.
I tried to use that smoking comb
and only burned my hair.
An African old wives' tale says
burnt hair drives you crazy,
says the head that owns your hair
won't let you own yourself,
will let you walk around in life living fantasies.
But what's an old wives' tale?

Part IV: Spring
I, too, wore locks before, but
if you have to force a style, is it natural?
Do not untwist, I'd say. Behave yourself
and stay.
But isn't it natural to let the dead hair shed,
like buried ancestors?
Holding on is no more natural
than letting go.
Freedom and choice should be what's natural.

With the freedom seeds of memory,
I choose to do what pleases me.

I, too, wore locks before—
doubly-conscious in a single style.
I was trying to be African American,
until I realized
I, too, am America,
out of Africa,
a collective consciousness,
even if I wear a blond wig.

My grandmothers earned me the right to grant
where to plant
the rooted strands,
like a past to relive
or just
to forgive.

LITERARY CRITICISM

He wanted a rite of passage so the beauty would be seen.

Beauty

Beauty is a judgment
that'll stab the night
to acquit a light
that blinds.

A fickle, inconstant decree,
a verdict,
a sentence,
a plea.

The Art of Solomon's Song

And I was a victim of your art
that confined me to a picture frame
and made me feel
ashamed
of what I was
outside the margins
of a present
not for me.

But the canvas is stretching out,
and I am moving past
the margins of re-creation, and
"behold, thou art fair, my love,
behold, thou art fair."
I am black,
but comely.

Trouble

Nobody knows
the trouble I've seen,
when written words
twisted
like cords in a rope
hang
to choke the words
of those lamb-like bodies
sacrificed, silenced
to swing and sing
no more.

Never Bound

You knew
that Clio fought Urania
for the opportunity
to gaze
on that which is forever before the eyes;

and bound Urania
in chains of cotton,
and blinded the eyes that knew
that cotton cannot bind
and stars are never bound
to any single gaze.

Classically,
you knew.

Right

He wanted to right
the couplets of Wheatley,
the folking of Hughes,
the dialect of Dunbar,
the preaching of Johnson,

when all the sounds were crowding out
the purpose of the sounding, so

he planted new criteria.
He wanted a rite
of passage so
the beauty would be seen despite
projected ugliness.

He would not be silenced, as
he brushed his voice
across the canvas of a zeitgeist
determined to predestine
a people as colored,
but uncolorful.

He wanted the right
to color everything
with words
that would be heard,
scraping words
like fingernails
across former miseducation
that confined thinking,
and acting,
and being.

The day for delusions was done.
He hung his words
at the front door
of progress.

PHILOSOPHY

Your words soared like flying swords.

Broad Sympathies

Your words soared
like flying swords
across a multitude of sympathies,
broad enough to trouble the land
like the oceans in the hands
of the omnipotent
moving upon the face of the waters,
until light exposed
firmaments
dividing divisions
and yet
uniting difference
into dissidence
that shook and mixed the disciplines
into
broad sympathies.

David: Spring

You stood as David
in this new
testament, Du Bois,
herding sheep
of youthful dreams,
counting years
like so many publications,
to make a name broadly in
science, literature, civil uplift,
redeeming time stolen
from ancestral grounds,
lest the sun set on your strength,
like bodies sinking into stolen waters
crossing middle passages.

David: Winter

You grew up
and out,
in favor and status,
gaining loves
and lovers,
casual indulgences,
rooftop beauties and
home-based duties;
basking in your modern ways,
a man before your time,
Victorian in decadent ways.

David: Fall

"But all
have fallen short,
and sinned."
Loving like an oasis
in a desert of deserted ladies,
when Fauset runs to another,
dripping with painful memories,
of sentiments sent
and returned,
no stamp of approval,
with strings detached and attached to another,
too tight to circulate,
too short to propagate.

And you, our David, continue to rule,
while families fall away
in matriarchal rivalry—
Yolande number one,
Yolande number two,
Yolande again,
with another man,
straight, yet crooked,
drinking and beating
long enough to make another
Yolande number three,
in reverse,
Daddy David.

David: Summer

Yet you,
heart after God,
produced a lineage,
outnumbering sands in hour-glasses,
paper-trails of publishing,
immortalizing ideologies,
babies produced asexually,
emasculated conception,
to save a race
replaced.

POLITICAL SCIENCE

...Where barbed wire pricks like cotton bolls....

Politics

You,
who dabbled in politics
and scored more than expected,
though not nearly
elected,
would cherish B. Obama, who
envisioned change
like the King you crowned
before transitioning
to the Motherland
and then
beyond.

Progress

As Daniel rebelled to excel
above
the typical status quo,
refusing to settle
for the king's meat,
you wielded pen
again and again,
like the staff of Moses,
to amuse yourself,
parting seas
that overflowed words of
arrogant oppressors pursuing
to re-enslave.

"In its place stood Progress;
and Progress," you insisted,
"is necessarily ugly."

Self-Segregation

Self-segregation
meant marching alongside progress,
boycotting
oppression suppressing
self-reliant
self-determination
into
self compliance.

But birds of a feather
flocked together
to block the locks
to the chains on change,
black on black on white crime
blocking progress
another time.

Self-Proclaimed

Me, myself, and I have lived
twice
before we started.
And history has given us
the seas
that never parted.

And I have tried to tell myself
that I depend on me
to bridge that past with future hope
to cross that biased sea.

For leaders have trod back and forth with rods,
with powerless rods,
and me, myself, and I have fought
amidst self-proclaimed gods.

I cannot leave myself behind
before I even start.
It's up to me to find the time
to make myself a part

of One who can speak to the sea
and calm the storm
raging
in me.

The New "N" Word

Disrespect is
the new "N" word,
in any shape or color,
the untitled,
first-name basis
camouflaging as friendship,
questioning credentials in friendly
conversation.
"Getting to know you,
getting to know all about you."
White is the reflection of all colors.
Black is the absorption of all colors.
Why capitalize the reflection of all colors
while lower casing all absorption
and lower casing class?
Capitalism is the cause of racism,
the unasked question, you said.

And Asante said,
"The African without Afrocentricity
is a matter of great concern,"

but the American,
without the African,
is a lesson too few learn.

And Asante said,
"There can be no hiding
from the agency of
awakened Africans."

Modern Alabama

Through Du Boisian eyes,
Alabama now has change,
but remains unchanged.
The recycled system looks different now.
Prisons loom like cotton
plantations,
where barbed wire pricks
like cotton bolls,
drawing blood like
knives that prick
inevitably;
humans drop like
flies
swatted down
to keep from disturbing those
behind the steering wheels
of black leadership
driving by;
wild flowers shooting up like weeds,
human weeds,
to be aborted,
as Sanger had intended—
with those surviving overseen
until big enough to be pulled and
imprisoned.

Overseers take over the children,
separating them from parents,
who were told
their sprouts were now old enough
to be pulled
like crops ready for harvesting.

Parents could not oversee
enough, for young crops belonged not
to black parentage, who,
sharecropping,
watched them only long enough
to wean them from all life,
until the seedlings held no roots.

In Modern Alabama,
where is the daybreak of Hughes,
with songs "rising out of the ground
like a swamp mist
and falling out of heaven like soft dew?"
The sorrow songs of a people
evaporated
into an endless sky,
trapped,
never to be anticipated,
or precipitated,
or reparated.
"A people thus handicapped
ought not to be asked to race
with the world,
but rather allowed to give
all its time
and thought
to its own social problems."
Cotton should be comfort,
not cold barbed wire.

ECONOMICS

...the mirage of change....

Change

And you stayed
on the battlefield
until you killed
the ideal
of a fair America,
until you marched across waters
in reverse middle passage,
squeezed between dead dreams
and diseased alliances
ceasing to hear
your voice.
The children you birthed
through voicing again and again
equality undivided
have grown up
to accommodate
the mirage of change.

Current Crisis

"If my people
who are called by my name,"
would see how
my name
has been used
again
for gain,
like currency,
stolen.
"Will a man rob God,"
who is against those
who oppress the hireling in his wages?"
Or will a man be God?

The record
of the darker races
serves
as testimony against the hypocrites
who dress in sheep's clothing,
to devour the profits
of recorded past.

Quick

Quick.
Quick money.
Fast cars. Easy life.

But speed is not as fast,
behind hard bars
     before hard scars
            beneath hard ground
with nothing left.

Quick.
Quick money.
Fast cars.
Easy death.

Cedar

We stumbled
into an open door,
the rug snatched out from under us,
when segregation ended.

The generation before,
accustomed to community,
tottered without the old foundation
that stood like cedar trees,
toughened through the years;
now cleared,
for a mall and cafeteria
and an indoor parking lot
for those who could not learn enough
to earn enough
outside the shade of cedar.

Such a Fire

Such a fire forced
the advancement of emancipation
for all people
eighty-seven years after
the people
declared independence.

Such a fire forced
the advancement of civil rights
for all people
one hundred years after
the people
allowed emancipation.

Now,
over fifty years later,
that fire
is still
advancing.

The Meaning of Progress

Change
constantly deferred
confers progress—
if progress
spells regress,
and backlash,
whipping like boomerangs,
failing to breach the wall.

DRAMA

...Like still-wet oil on canvas....

What I Know

I don't suspect that I could love a tree
whose branches reach and span the width of me,
and if I thought that I could someday see
the winds that make the leaves fall from the tree,
I could let go of much that uproots me.

I do not think the tree is meant to know
that others watch and make sure it will grow,
and that the wind will blow when it will blow,
a wind that that old tree may never know,
and that the growth is painful and so slow.

And that is why I cannot love a tree
that makes me think of what I ought to be,
for when I think that life is what I know,
that is when the winds begin to blow.

Act One

W. E. B. Du Bois,
a Jeremiad in Black
face,
slowly dancing,
with a big white frown,
crying before
Whites amused
by Christian politics.

Act Two

W. E. B. Du Bois,
front and
center stage,
foremost,
a prophet for the promise,
smile drawn on
with pen that struck thoughts,
like lightening,
the same spot,
more than once.

Forgiven

And you recycled words
again and again,
never wasting a thought,
resurrecting piece after piece,
like grandmothers
who jellied peels
and pickled watermelon rinds.
Like you, they knew
to use it all,
from pickled feet
to scrambled brain,
squeezing the intestines of hogs
despite the stench,
wasting not to want not,
in a day when days were different.
Now, all seems commonplace,
and we buy hog chitterlings
in a Piggly Wiggly bucket
and pay,
assigning fancy names for all,
like tripe and souse,
like scholars who quote themselves
extensively, copiously,
with credits acknowledged
or not, but
forgiven.

Afrocentric Butterflies

Fields of dreams
tilled to bloom for butterflies
escape cocoons of circumstance
and nourish caterpillars
too low to know the growth
of dreams too tough to die.

Caterpillars fed on dreams
and grew,
escaping cocoons,
to bloom
Afrocentricly
for they were made
to fly.

Myself

I celebrate the mountains of myself.
Their tops, unsettling to see,
provoke in me an aim
that sends me soaring
like a bird for the horizon.

I celebrate the seed trees of myself
that grow and sow and grow again
sending my heart yearning
for fertile ground of living.

I celebrate the keyboards of myself
that tap
from single units
new impressions,
known before shown and
ready for release,
like still wet oil on canvas.

Almost a Century

After almost a century,
you embraced Africa.

Mourning a new America,
you yearned for the old mother,
like a baby craving milk,
you returned to the womb
of a culture giving birth.

The eldest sibling,
the first-born,
the U.S.A. of another day,
refused to hear your plea
for just a taste of heritage.
What would your final essay say?
Through you, essays,
time and time again,
would say not nearly enough to change the immutable.

You,
who pitied Crummell for working alone,
with "little human sympathy,"
fled the U. S. A.
like a canon shot in a war,
a civil war,
uncivil.

Four-score and ten and a half years,
you, too, "wandered in this same world" as his.
Crummell earned your accolades,
as you "bowed before this man,
as one bows before the prophets of the world."

Nine decades
wrapped around a world of idle worship,
wanting to inform
the norm,
the tenth left off this time,
like the top of a candle wick
Never to be burned again.